Machine Learning

Introduction to Supervised and Unsupervised Learning Algorithms with Real-World Applications

Morgan Maynard

Table of Contents

2

Chapter 1 – Introduction to Machine Learning

To make any computer program work, you must build a set of instructions that tell it exactly what to do; these are called the *code*. Here you must carefully define every input, every calculation and every output; this occurs because computers cannot figure things out on their own. You can write thousands of lines of code perfectly, but even if there is a comma missing your program will crash.

In these occasions a person must read the code, assess what the problems are, identify the missing comma and insert it – this process is called *debugging*. Why can't computers do this process by themselves? Simple, because no one programmed them to. The ability to analyze new scenarios and adapt to changing situations is called *learning*. It is only found in intelligent creatures, not computers.

Machine Learning is a branch of computer science that wants to change this paradigm altogether and close the gap between human and computer behavior. Machine Learning wants to stop giving computers detailed instructions and instead provide them with a high level, broad set of guidelines which can adapt to many different scenarios – these are called **algorithms**. In practice, they want to give computers the ability to **learn** and to **adapt**.

These algorithms enable computers to gain insights, recognize patterns and make predictions from data, images, sounds or videos we have never seen before (or even knew existed). Unfortunately, the true power and applications of today's Machine Learning Algorithms is misunderstood by most people.

Through this book I want solve this confusion, I want to shed light on the most relevant Machine Learning Algorithms used in the industry and describe what these algorithms can achieve. I will start by discussing simple machine learning algorithms based on predictive statistical modelling such as KNN and Regressions. As the book progresses and your understanding of the field expands, we will dive into more advanced algorithms based on adaptive learning such as Support Vector Machines, Naïve Bayes and Neural Networks. For each algorithm covered in this book I will discuss how it works, why it works and when you should use it. All algorithms are supported by real-life examples worked through in an easy-to-follow step-by-step fashion.

Chapter 2 - About the Series

"Machine Learning: Introduction to Supervised and Unsupervised Learning Algorithms with Real-World Applications" is the first instalment of the book series **Advanced Data Analytics**, carefully developed by myself and a team of software-loving engineers. This series will provide you with an introduction into the world of modern data analytics. The material covered is roughly comparable to a 1-semester introductory course at Undergraduate College Level. You can find all my books and future releases on my official Amazon Author Page.

Throughout the series I will only assume a high-school level knowledge in mathematics and statistics and no previous exposure to computing or coding. Whenever we will come across a new topic, concept or formula I will make sure to cover all the required material beforehand, maximizing and facilitating your learning process.

However, my explanations can only go *so far*. Please understand this series will challenge and push your understanding of the modern tech world, revealing many applications of computer and algorithms you never thought possible. Especially in later books, we will dive into very technical topics at the forefront of research. To follow along and keep up with the material, you must be **committed** and **passionate** about the topics we will cover.

The material across the three-book series was designed to work in synergy and therefore I recommend reading across all 3 books for the most complete learning experience. I would highly appreciate any feedback on the current publications and suggestions for future topics – please leave these in Amazon's official review section.

If you are ready, let's begin your journey into the world of Machine Learning.

Chapter 3 – Supervised vs Unsupervised Learning Algorithms

If you want a machine learning algorithm to solve a problem, you must train it. Unlike humans, you do not teach a machine in a classroom; you teach machines using **training data**. Fundamentally, training data are past examples showing the machine how to solve a problem. Using your chosen algorithm, the machine works through all these examples and *understands* how to solve them. If you use a few very specific examples, the machine will only be able to solve very similar problems. If you use very large and broad training data, your machine will learn how to solve a wide range of diverse problems.

Think of yourself as the machine and training data as textbooks. If you read a lot of textbooks you will gain a lot of knowledge, which you can use to solve a wide range of problems. You can make connection between the different books and attempt challenges you have never seen before. If you read only a few textbooks, you do not have much knowledge. You can only solve a few, similar problems to what you have come across already. Machine Learning is exactly like that!

Although there are many different machine learning algorithms you can use, these can all be divided into two main categories: **supervised learning** and **unsupervised learning.**

Supervised Learning

The only difference between supervised and unsupervised learning lies in the type of training data you use. In supervised learning you provide **labelled** training data. This means that each example you feed into your algorithm is classified into a recognizable data class or type. If this is the first time reading about labelled training data, it may appear confusing. Do not panic, an example will make everything clear once again.

Think of yourself trying to learn a new language, let's say Italian; your teacher gives you training data in form of vocabulary. This data is labelled because each new word you learn is classified into recognizable terms. For instance, your teacher tells you "ciao" means "hello" in English, she tells you "mangiare" means "eating", etc... Each example of a new Italian word has been associated into an English word you can understand. This is labelled data because each data entry is, effectively labelled. Supervised learning works the same way.

Unsupervised Learning

Unsupervised learning occurs through **unclassified** or **unlabeled** training data; this can be a trickier concept to understand because we do it subconsciously. For example, you can think of it as learning through observations rather than from a book.

To clarify this concept, let's jump back to the example of someone who is learning Italian by watching movies and listening to podcasts in the language. If you don't know any Italian and you watch a movie you will not understand anything. Second movie – nothing, third movie – still nothing. After ten movies you might start to recognize common expressions, for instance every time a character says "Arrivederci" you observe someone leave and you conclude this means "goodbye".

If you watch thousands of movies you would learn how to speak Italian perfectly using this technique, you would simply "pick it up". Clearly, you can't do that because it's too time consuming for you - **but not for a computer.** You could acquire millions of hours of Italian speech and run them all through a machine learning algorithm. After "listening and learning" to all these hours of Italian, the computer will have mastered the meaning of the language.

Hence, unsupervised learning is defined by **unclassified** training data. You provide a machine with thousands of problems and their results, but you do not explain how the result is calculated. The algorithm then starts to look for things in common; it tries to identify shared traits and features between the problems and the solutions. With enough data, the algorithm will identify patterns and develop a strategy to solve the problem. This is how unsupervised algorithms can teach computers using unclassified training data.

Chapter 4 – Classification vs Regression

Before diving into the details and applications of each algorithm, we must discuss the differences between classification and regression – two key concepts in the field of machine learning.

Based on my industrial experience in computational analytics, over 80% of the models I have come across were **classification models** while only 15-20% were **regression models**. This bias in favor of classification is by no means unique to my experience or work. Classification models are more common throughout the machine learning industry at large. Now you might ask, why are classification models so strongly favored over regression models? First, let's distinguish between classification and regression models:

Classification models: the results of a classification problem will fall into *class labels* (i.e. results fall into clearly defined boundaries/categories/groups). An example of this problem might be predicting the next color of the roulette table. There are only three clearly-defined options: red, black or green. There is no intermediate answer, there is no half-way output; the answer can only be one of the three options – these are ***three class labels***.

Regression models: the problem result can have a *continuous value*. An example of this problem is trying to predict the weight of the next egg produced in a chicken farm. There are no defined choices or classes for the weight of an egg; it can weigh 54.3g, 87.3g or 62.9 – it is a *continuous value.*

Now that I have defined the two types of models, we can return to the original question: *why are classification models preferred over regression models within the data analysis industry?* The reason for this bias links to the fundamental purpose of machine learning algorithms: **helping users make a decision**.

In fact - as machine learning engineers and data analysts – we are looking for well-structured answers that clearly tell us what decision to take. For instance, let's consider the following problem: "**should I advertise on a given online platform**?" A regression model would reply "*platform viewers are 13% likely to buy your product*", whereas a classification model might reply "yes - *the viewer's characteristics match your target audience based on your chosen parameters*". Which answer do you think is more useful? Which helps us make decisions? Which can we most effectively apply into the real world? Clearly, classification models are the most effective to make decisions and hence why they are chosen.

However, we must understand that classification models, in spite the most common, are imperfect approximation of a chaotic world. In fact, we live in a disorganized world and clearly-defined structures rarely come by. This means we tend to **rationalize** imperfect and continuous problems into what I refer to as *classification buckets*. These are artificial boundaries or classes that help data analysts organize and structure natural, messy and unclear data into manageable and organized data that is easy to read, understand and can help us make decisions. The effectiveness and usefulness of a classification problem all depends on how the classification buckets have been chosen.

For instance, predicting the conversion rate of a particular customer stream is clearly regression problem – is it 1%, 5%, 8.3234%? But if you create classification buckets that breakdown the conversion rate into: 0-5% (or "low conversion"), 6-10% (or "medium conversion"), 11-15% (or "high conversion"), then you find yourself dealing with a classification problem. The results are an approximate representation of the real problem. However, what you obtain is more structured, easier to read, interpret and understand. You can present these results to your colleagues or the marketing team and they will **help**

Chapter 5 – K-Nearest Neighbor

The K-NN algorithm is one of the simplest machine learning algorithms used by today's data scientists. It was first developed for statistical prediction and pattern recognition in the early 1970's and can be applied to both regression and classification problems, although it is most commonly applied to classification models.

How does it work?

Whenever making predictions, KNN must access the entire set of training data available. This means no learning is required as all data must be stored in memory and remain always accessible. If you are dealing with large datasets, you may want to consider complex data structures, such as k-d trees, to maximize storage efficiency and computational speeds.

For each new data point, KNN searches through all the training data for the K closest entries (nearest neighbors). K is the number of neighbors considered by the algorithm – when k=1 only the closest value will be considered, for k = 3 the three closest values will be considered, for k = infinity the entire dataset will be considered, etc.

Once the k closest data points are identified (K-nearest neighbors) their properties and values are assessed. A function (discussed later) will consider all of these properties and compute an output value for the new data point. For regressions the predicted value might be the weighted average of the nearest neighbors, for classification it may be the most frequent class.

Distances or degree of separation between the new data point and its neighbors must also be considered. For instance, if 2 "squares" neighbors are **closer** than 3 "strawberry" neighbors the predicted class of the new entry point may be "squares". Of course, this depends on how you *define* **distances** in your dataset (for now, you can think of distance as a measure of error).

Before diving into the concept of **distance** and discuss the different metrics available, let's visualize what was discussed this far. In the following figure you will find a training data set for two classes of data: squares and diamonds. The two variables that define these points are: Loan$ and Age – these are called the **predictors.**

Using this data set, a KNN algorithm can be used to predict the class of a new data point i.e. should the circle be a square or a diamond? In this particular example I have chosen k = 4 for my KNN algorithm. Now, I must select the 4 nearest neighbors to the new data point, i.e. the circle.

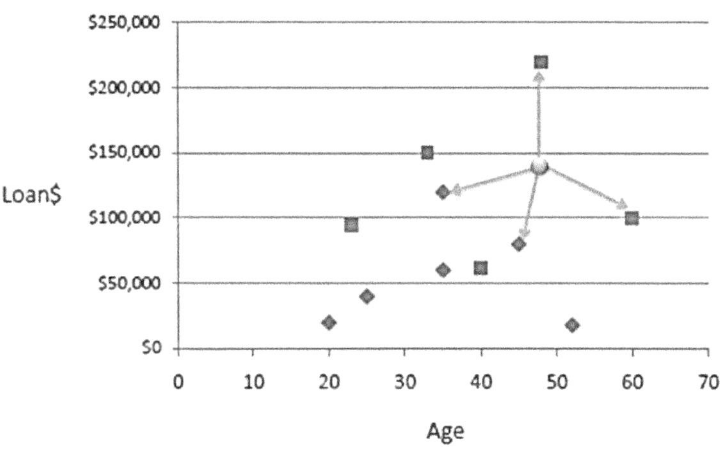

As you can see, 2 of the closest neighbors are diamonds and 2 are squares – what class should we assign to the circle? This will depend on how your algorithm defines the 'distance' parameter. For instance, if you consider absolute distance (i.e. how far the point is on the graph from the training data) then your algorithm will predict 'diamond' because the 2 diamonds are closer. However, if age is a more important factor to your study, you may choose to give it a greater weighting factor w (discussed later). Hence, your 'distance' is more biased towards minimize difference in age and will predict 'square' (because the squares are closer in age to the circle). **Distance** is a key parameter for any KNN algorithm - it must be chosen and tuned carefully based on the needs of your study.

When specifying 'distance' metrics for your algorithm, a few things must be kept in mind. First, you must select the most relevant predictors (i.e. age and loan in the previous example).

Due to differences in scale between predictors it is common practice to normalize them to values between 0-1. For instance, in the example above you would have loan\$ in the range of 60,000-250,000 and the age ranging 20-52; these discrepancies in scale must be factored into how your algorithm will deal with 'distances' between training data.

If you want to assign a greater factor of importance to a chosen predictor, you can use a **weight factor w** after normalizing the data. For example, now your data will range from 0 to 1*w (the weight factor). The greater the weight factor, the greater impact a predictor will have on determining the final output. Choosing the predictors and weight factors that give maximum accuracy is called *parameter tuning*. There is no right or wrong way to do this – it depends on many factors – the best way remains trial and error.

Although this process may appear confusing and even random at first, with experience you will learn to tune parameters quickly and effortlessly to an algorithm that works for your data and your requirements– it just takes practice.

Once you have selected and weighted the predictors, you must now choose how the 'distance' parameter is calculated. The most common approach is using **Euclidian distance** – if you do not have prior experience in machine learning I highly recommend you use this technique. It is a very effective and straightforward technique, regularly used throughout the industry. The mathematical formula to compute the Euclidian distance is shown on the following page.

$$\sqrt{\sum_{i=1}^{k}\left(x_i - y_i\right)^2}$$

Other distance measures that can be implemented into KNN are mentioned below. Due to the broad range of subjects covered in this book, I will only briefly mention these other metrics. Of course, there are more distance metrics that can be implemented – you can even create a bespoke distance function yourself to suit your predictors perfectly. Like many aspects of machine learning algorithms, a lot comes down to parameter tuning.

- **Hamming Distance** – useful when dealing with binary vectors (i.e. classes)

- **Manhattan Distance** – use the sum of the absolute difference between data vectors to calculate distance

- **Minkowsky Distance** – A combination of Manhattan and Euclidian distances.

With regards to the optimum value for K, again there is no right answer. Parameter tuning and experimenting is required to identify what works best for your training data and your individual needs. However, do keep in mind that large values of K will have longer computational times. The particular impact of this depends on the complexity of your algorithm, size of data set and computational power available.

Another key concern when dealing with KNN algorithm is **scale**, particularly relating to the size of your training data. Remember that, in order to make a prediction, the algorithm must access each entry in the training data and search for the k most similar values (the nearest neighbors). If your training data consists of hundreds of thousands of entries, analyzing each point means significant challenges in computational time and storage space.

An effective solution is using a **stochastic subset of data**. This means that, if your training data has 100,000 entries, you build your KNN algorithm using only 1,000 randomly selected points. This is usually a good work-around large datasets. You can drastically reduce computational time and retain a good level of accuracy - especially when there is a lot of repetition in your training data. To choose an appropriate size of the stochastic subset, I tend to run trials and compare the results against the entire data set. You will find that as subset size decreases so does the accuracy of your prediction. Based on your computational time and accuracy requirements, select a minimum threshold discrepancy (e.g. 95%) and then choose the smallest subset size that matches this. Be sure to run this test for multiple entries to avoid any outliers.

Preparing your training data for KNN

Preparing and filtering training data before running any machine learning algorithm can drastically improve predictive power, accuracy and efficiency. When implementing a KNN, you should always:

- **Rescale the predictors:** Always try to normalize your predictors so they fall between values of 0 and 1.

- **Remove missing data:** If a data point is missing (i.e. has a value of zero) it can cause severe damage to the 'distance' calculations. All zero data should be removed from the training data.

- **Reduce number of entries:** As already explained, KNN must access and examine all entries in your training data set. If this contains 100,000 points, high computational power will be required. By using a **stochastic subset** (for instance 1,000 randomly selected points) you can greatly reduce computational requirements, often with minimal effect on accuracy.

Final Remarks

The KNN algorithm is a simple machine learning algorithm capable of delivering highly competitive results. This model requires access to all training data sets, as it does not carry out a *learning* process. It is a perfect choice for newcomers to machine learning algorithms or those looking to build a predictive model quickly. In spite of its inherent simplicity, there are many variations and parameters you can tune to maximize predictive accuracy and computational speed. Please keep in mind there is no single most effective set up, as with most machine learning algorithms you will have to experiment and tune all parameters using a trial-and-error approach that best suits your training data.

Chapter 6 – Naive Bayes

Naïve Bayes is a popular machine learning algorithm that uses statistical modelling to tackle *classification* problems. In spite of its relative simplicity, Naïve Bayes can deliver a high level of accuracy when used correctly. Naïve Bayes is highly scalable compared to today's most complex machine learning algorithms, such as *Support Vector Machines* (see chapter 8).

How does it work?

This algorithm is built on Bayes' Theorem under a fundamental assumption: *all predictors are independent from each other*. Unlike KNN, Naïve Bayes does not store training data. The algorithm studies the training data, it learns from it and the classification model adapts.

This may sound confusing, so let's dive into an example:

We will now explore how Naïve Bayes can be used to classify an unknown fruit into one of three classes: **apples, oranges** and **strawberries.** The predictors available for the new fruit are: **color, shape** and **size.** The information for a new, unknown fruit is presented below – how will Naïve Bayes help determine if it is an orange, apple or strawberry? Let's see…

Predictors	Unknown Fruit
Color	Red
Shape	Round
Size	Diameter = 3 inches

While in real life the predictors depend on each another, Naïve Bayes considers them completely independent features (hence, the use of the word 'naïve'). The model assigns a probability that *each* predictor belongs to a given class independently of other features – this is known as the *class-predictor probability*.

First the color of the fruit is considered – **'Red'**. The algorithm *knows* this color is commonly found in apples and strawberries, but rarely in oranges. The shape is then assessed – **'Round'**. Your computational model *knows* apples and oranges are typically round, whereas strawberries are not. Finally, the fruit size is considered – **'diameter = 3 inches'**. The predictive model *knows* that apples are more likely to have this size than oranges, (which are typically larger) or strawberries (which are typically smaller). Hence, the model assigns a probability that each predictor belongs to a given class, as shown below:

Predictors	Unknown Fruit	Probability of Apple	Probability of Orange	Probability of Strawberry
Colour	Red	40%	0%	60%
Shape	Round	42%	56%	2%
Size	Diameter=3 inches	65%	34%	1%

Predictor-class probabilities contribute towards the final model output using a mathematical function which is chosen by the data analyst. You can multiply, average, sum, find the least square difference - I recommend a **weighted multiplication** function. To do this you must first assign a **weight factor w** (see chapter 4) to each predictor – this is an arbitrary value assigned by you that represents how relevant this predictor is to your study; you can optimize this value through *parameter tuning*. Afterwards, the likelihood of a class is given by the *sum of each predictor-class percentage multiplied by its weight.* The mathematical formula is shown below:

Likelihood of class = Sum (P(predictor) x weight)

Please note the notation P(predictor) indicates the predictor-class percentage. I have reported the completed table for the previous example below. I assigned a higher weight to **shape** because I think it is the most *unique* feature of a fruit and therefore I think it is the **most useful** to predict the fruit class. As you can see, the predictor weight is a purely arbitrary parameter chosen by the analyst.

Predictors	Weight	Unknown Fruit	Probability of Apple	Probability of Orange	Probability of Strawberry
Colour	2	Red	40%	0%	60%
Shape	3	Round	42%	56%	2%
Size	2	Diameter=3 inches	65%	34%	1%
		Likelihood of class	**3.4**	**2.4**	**1.8**

The model predicts that the unknown fruit of color red, round shape and a 3-inch diameter is an apple, not a strawberry or an orange. This decision was made by choosing the fruit class with the highest predicted likelihood of class. This result seems an accurate prediction made by the model.

Origin of the class-predictor probability

While working through the previous example you probably wondered "where is the training data being used?" In the second chapter I have stressed the *need for* training data in all machine learning algorithms, and yet there was no reference to it in the example above?

You may also have asked yourself where the predictor-class percentages come from. How did I know that a red fruit is 40% likely to be an apple, 0% likely to be an orange and 60% likely to be a strawberry? How did I know that a fruit with a 3 inch is 65% likely to be an apple, 34% likely to be an orange and 1% likely to be a strawberry?

The two questions above are related: the class-predictor percentages in fact come directly from the training data.

More precisely, when building my fruit-classification model I used all the training data available to **teach** my algorithm about fruit. My fruit-classification algorithm *'studied'* all the information in the training data and **learned** the properties of the fruits. By studying this data, it learned that if a fruit is red it has a 60% chance of being an apple, etc... Hence, it extracted the predictor-class percentages.

Now we are starting to explore the powers associated with **learning**. Think back to the KNN algorithm discussed in the previous chapter – every time it did a new calculation it had to revisit all of the training data to extract old information, because it did not learn. It did not have ability to understand information and remember it for a later use. This imposed a lot of limitations – the algorithm was slow and memory-intensive; you simply cannot revisit 10,000 data points for every prediction.

Through learning, Naïve Bayes changes all of this. The training data is visited only once when building the model, the first time. Once the class predictor probabilities are obtained, the training data is not needed anymore, providing gains in computational speed and memory requirements.

Learning from training data

In the previous section I have explained that Naïve Bays *learns* from your training data and that, because of this, it reaps massive efficiency and speed gains over the KNN algorithm. But what exactly did *learning* mean? Or more precisely, how did it derive the class predictor probabilities? How did it learn that 40% of the red fruits were red? Let's explore:

The most advanced machine learning algorithms learn from training data by fitting exponential coefficients using complicated mathematical optimization procedures. These algorithms require a lot of computational power and are often limited in scale (i.e. size of training data set). Naïve Bayes takes a more fundamental approach to learning, making it easy, fast and scalable.

In more detail, let's analyze how the Naïve Bayes algorithm learns from a training dataset using the earlier example: the fruit classifier model.

To simplify the example, I will work through the learning process with only 1 predictor (color) and a small training data set of only 19 entries. In reality, Naïve Bayes models are built with thousands or more entries and multiple predictors. The larger the data set, the better accuracy the algorithm will have.

Step 1 – Raw Training data

In the first step you must obtain and store your training data in a clear, structured format. For each class (in my case fruit) you must have a corresponding predictor value (in my case colour). Please note this is a classification problem, therefore the predictor must fall into clearly-cut, separated *classes.* The predictor cannot be of continuous value – if so, you must establish *classification buckets* as you see most appropriate (see chapter 3).

Class (Fruit)	Predictor 1 (Colour)
Apple	Green
Orange	Orange
Apple	Red
Strawberry	Red
Apple	Red
Orange	Orange
Orange	Orange
Strawberry	Red
Strawberry	Red
Strawberry	Yellow
Strawberry	Red
Apple	Yellow
Orange	Orange
Apple	Red
Strawberry	Red
Strawberry	Red
Orange	Orange
Orange	Orange
Apple	Red

Step 2 – Build a Predictor-frequency table

You must then build a predictor frequency table. The purpose of this table is to record *how many times* a predictor occurs for each class. The predictor-frequency for the earlier training data is shown on the following page:

	COLOUR (PREDICTOR CLASS)			
FRUIT	Red	Yellow	Green	Orange
Apple	4	1	1	0
Orange	0	0	0	0
Strawberry	6	1	0	6
Total	**10**	**2**	**1**	**6**

Step 3 – Calculate predictor-class percentages

You can now calculate the probability that a given predictor belongs to given class, this is called the *predictor-class* probability. In statistics, this term is defined using the following notation P(class|predictor). For example, if a fruit is red it has a 60% probability of being an apple – this can be noted as P(Apple|Red) = 60%.

	PREDICTOR-CLASS PERCENTAGES			
FRUIT	Red	Yellow	Green	Orange
Apple	60%	50%	100%	0
Orange	0	0	0	0
Strawberry	40%	50%	0	100%

Chapter 7 – Logistic Regression

Introduction

Logistic Regression is a popular algorithm for **binary classification** problems – i.e. the outcome can only take one of two values, also known as a dichotomy. For instance, will it rain tomorrow? Will the coin fall on head or tails? Will my airplane arrive to destination before 10.00am? All these problems have only **two possible answers:** yes and no.

Before we can discuss logistic regression algorithms in detail, you must understand how linear regression works. In particular, you must become familiar with the idea of a **best-fit line** - a fundamental concept in the field of statistics. If you are unfamiliar with the topic or would appreciate a refresher, fear not – I will cover everything you need in the following sections.

Background Knowledge – Linear Regression

The fundamental idea behind linear regression is the *linear* dependency between predictors. In other words, the training data follows a straight-line trend when plotted on a graph. As a data analyst your task is to find the line that best models this linear trend, also known as the line of **best-fit**.

Take a look at the following example: I have plotted a set of training data and the corresponding line of best fit. In practice, we are trying to model a linear path that best 'predicts' the path or position of our data points. Please, also notice that, in linear regression, our predictors take on a numerical and continuous value.

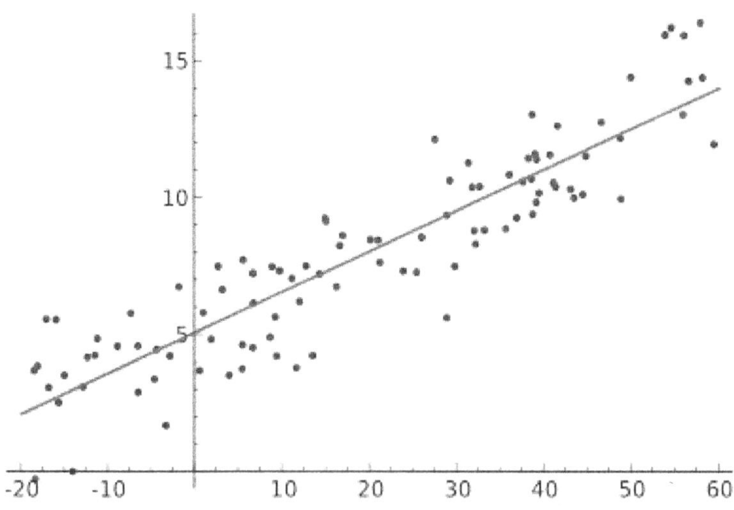

Background Knowledge - Finding the line of best fit

Finding the equation of the best-fit line is a very straightforward procedure when dealing with linera regression problems. First, we must consider the mathematical equation of the best-fit line:

$$y = ax + b$$

In the above equation the term 'x' represents the predictor of our data (plotted on the horizontal axis), whereas the term 'y' represents the outcome (plotted on the vertical axis). The terms **a** and **b** determine the shape and positioning of our best-fit line – they are called **coefficients**. More precisely:

- **a** – defines the **slope** of the best-fit line (i.e. how steep it is)
- **b** – defines the y-intercept of the best-fit line (i.e. shift the line vertically)

Now that we know how to define the shape/position of our best-fit line (i.e. by changing our coefficients). How can we find the line that best matches/models/tracks our data?

The standard industry practice is to use the **Least Squares Method**. The objective of this method is to *minimize the total distance between the line and the training data*. In other words, you are finding the line that passes **closest** to all your data.

To find this 'closest' line, a process of mathematical optimization is carried out on the line's coefficients **a** and **b**, until the total distance between the line and all of the training data is minimized. There is no need to dive into the mathematical equation for the LSE or the optimization methodology – a broad understanding for linear regression is sufficient. We can now move onto logistic regression.

How does Logistic Regression work?

Logistic Regression forms part of a much larger family of algorithms known as the Generalized Linear Model (GLM). These were developed by Nelder and Wedderburn in 1972, who were trying to apply the principles of linear regression to new and more complex problems. In fact, logistic regression represents a direct derivative of linear regression – let's analyze how.

In linear regression you are trying to model the final **value** of your outcome – i.e. the 'y' variable. However, in logistic regression you are dealing with binary problems – i.e. there is no value to predict, the problem only has two possible solutions. Your goal is to predict the **probability** that an event will occur, i.e. how likely an instance will be.

An example of a linear regression problem is: *"how many millimetres of rainfall there will be in Alabama tomorrow?"* – You are looking for a **value**. In logistic regression you would consider a very different type of problem, for instance: *"will it rain in New York tomorrow?"* – there are only two answers to this question "yes" or "no", hence a binary classification problem. A logistic regression algorithm will provide the answer in form of a percentage, i.e. *"there is a 76% chance that it will rain in New York tomorrow".*

Now, let's think back to our best-fit line: in linear regression we were trying to model our predictors using a straight line (assumption of linear dependency).

In logistic regression we work under the assumption of a *natural probabilistic occurrence*, mathematically known as the natural logarithm. Hence, instead of mapping our data to straight-line, we use the **sigmoid function** also known as a logistic function or s-function – shown on the following page.

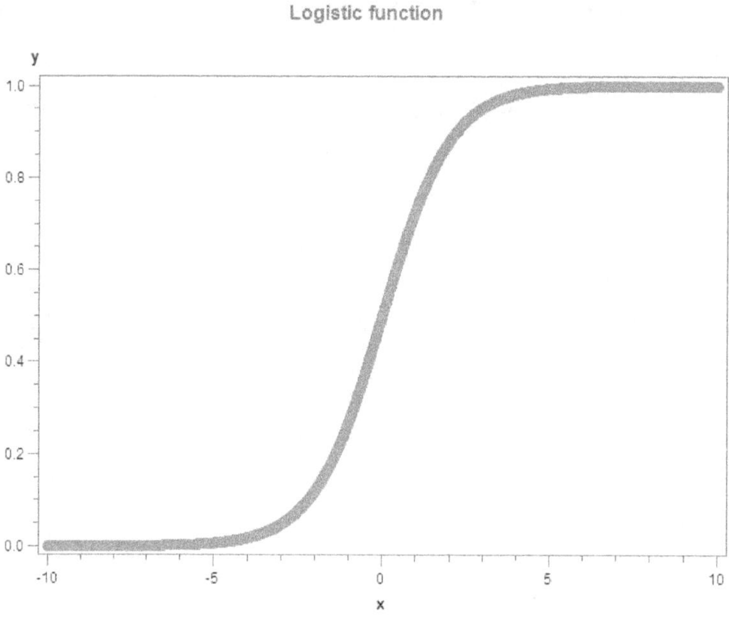

As seen in the graph, the sigmoid function ranges in value between 0 and 1, but never reaching those exact limits - mathematicians call these *asymptotes*. In logistic regression, we are using this line to represent binary probabilities. Hence the boundary of 0 means *an event will never occur* and the boundary of 1 means *an event will surely occur*. Everything in between has a given chance of happening, for instance a value of 0.2 means there is a 20% chance a binary event will take place.

Learning from training data

As we already saw with the Naïve Bayes algorithm in the previous chapter, also the Logistic Regression algorithm must 'study' from the training data available and 'learn' from it. In the context of Logistic Regression 'learning' occurs by best-fitting the sigmoid function to match our training data. This process is very similar to optimizing a best-fit line in linear regression discussed earlier. First, let's analyze the equation of a sigmoid function:

$$P = \frac{1}{1 + e^{-(a + bx)}}$$

This equation is significantly more complex than previously discussed in linear regression, but there are similarities nonetheless. You will notice the variable '**x**' – this represents the predictor plotted on the horizontal axis. You will also notice the equation coefficients **a** and **b** – these determine the shape and positioning of the Sigmoid function. More specifically:

> **a** – controls horizontal shift of the sigmoid-function (i.e. moves the curve left and right)

b – controls the steepness of the slope of the sigmoid-function (i.e. how steep the curve is)

We now know how to control the shape and positioning of the Sigmoid function – how do we find the best-fit to our training data?

In linear regression we use a process called the Least Squares Method; this minimizes the distance between the straight line and the training data. But in logistic regression we are working with percentages not values, therefore we must us a different method: this is called **Maximum Likelihood Estimation**. The objective of this method is to *find the Sigmoid function that will match the predictions made by our training data as closely as possible.* In other words, we are no longer looking for the closest values; we are now looking for the closest predictions.

A mathematical optimization process is carried out on the function's coefficients **a** and **b**. Numerous iterations are tested until the sigmoid function with the predictions closest to our training data is found. Once we obtain the best-fit sigmoid function, we can say our algorithm has successfully 'learned' from all the training data and can now make effective predictions based on it.

Take a look at the sample probabilities below. Note how the logistic regression algorithm has 'learned' from the training data. Based on this new s-function, I can now make predictions using one single predictor (in the horizontal axis).

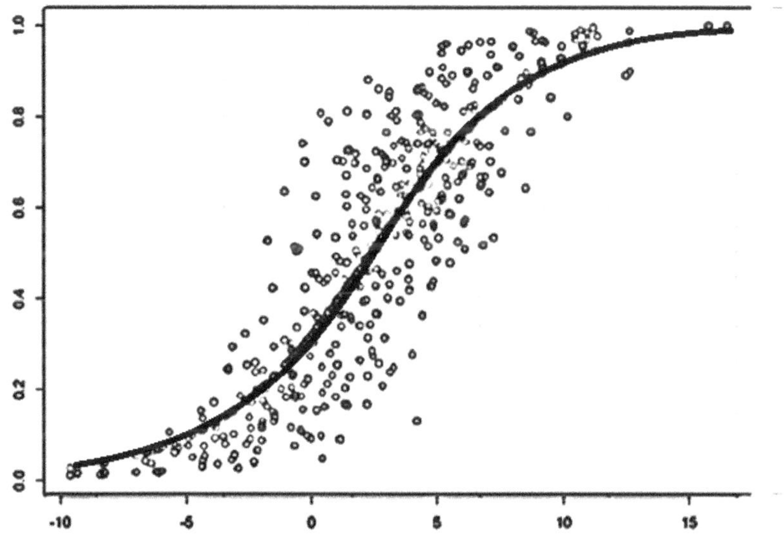

Chapter 8 –Decision Trees

Introduction

Decision Tree algorithms are used to develop *classification* models in the form of a tree structure. They are extremely popular amongst today's analysts and, when used correctly, they can achieve good accuracy and stability.

These algorithms boast a very unique property: they are extremely easy to read and understand. In fact, they are one of the only machine learning models that are *interpretable*. In other words, you can see and understand exactly why the classifier makes a decision. For those of you with less experience coding or developing machine learning models, this feature will prove very valuable.

How Does it Work?

All Decision Tree algorithms follow the same strategy: *breakdown a dataset into smaller and smaller subsets based on the available predictors. The goal is to obtain subsets that contain only one class of outcomes.* This may sound confusing, so I will guide you through an example before covering any additional theory.

Example

In this example I will use the Decision Tree algorithm to predict whether John will play tennis or not based on the weather. Here is the training data available:

Predictors			Outcome
Sky	**Humidity**	**Wind**	**John Plays Tennis?**
Sunny	High	Low	No
Sunny	High	High	No
Overcast	High	Low	Yes
Rain	High	Low	Yes
Rain	Low	Low	Yes
Rain	Low	High	No
Overcast	Low	High	Yes
Sunny	High	Low	No
Sunny	Low	Low	Yes
Rain	Low	Low	Yes
Sunny	Low	High	Yes
Overcast	High	High	Yes
Overcast	Low	Low	Yes
Rain	High	High	No

Split into first subsets according to predictor

Your first step is to split the data based on the predictors available. Remember your goal: *group all outcomes of a single class together.* I have chosen to split the training set according to the 'sky' predictor, as shown on the next page.

In the above diagram you will notice how 3 subsets have been created according to the 'sky' predictor. We can immediately start to make some conclusions, for instance *John always plays when the sky is overcast* **or** *there is a 60% chance John will play tennis when it rains.*

Further Splits

Let's reconsider our main objective: *create subsets with only one class of data*, this was achieved for only one subset. In fact, all outcomes in the 'Overcast' subset are of the same class (a 'Yes' only) and therefore this subset should not be split further. However, the two remaining subsets contain outcomes of mixed class and therefore should be split further, as shown in the following page:

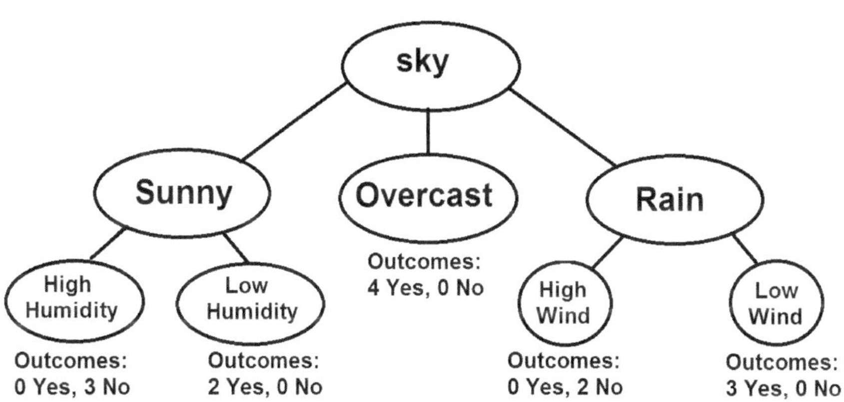

The tree-based model above is now complete – all subsets contain only 1 class type, i.e. either all 'yes' or all 'no'. Also notice that I have split the 'Sunny' and 'Rain' subsets with different predictors. After some quick analysis I noticed that 'humidity' would give perfect classes for the subset 'Sunny'. However, the 'wind' predictor produces perfect classes for the subset 'Rain'.

The above tree based model is also very useful to *analyse* John's behaviour. For instance, we immediately see that *John never plays when it's sunny and very humid* **or** *he never plays when it's Rainy and very windy.* Clearly, Decision Tree classification models are very easy to read and can provide immediate feedback.

Making a prediction using the above tree

In the earlier example I trained a *classification* model using a basic decision tree algorithm. This model predicts if John will play tennis or not based on the current whether conditions. So, let's immediately put it into practice: *today's weather conditions are listed below, will John play tennis?*

Sky	Humidity	Wind	John Plays Tennis?
Rain	Low	Low	No

Making a prediction using a tree-based classification model is extremely simple; we must simply follow the path that matches all our predictors:

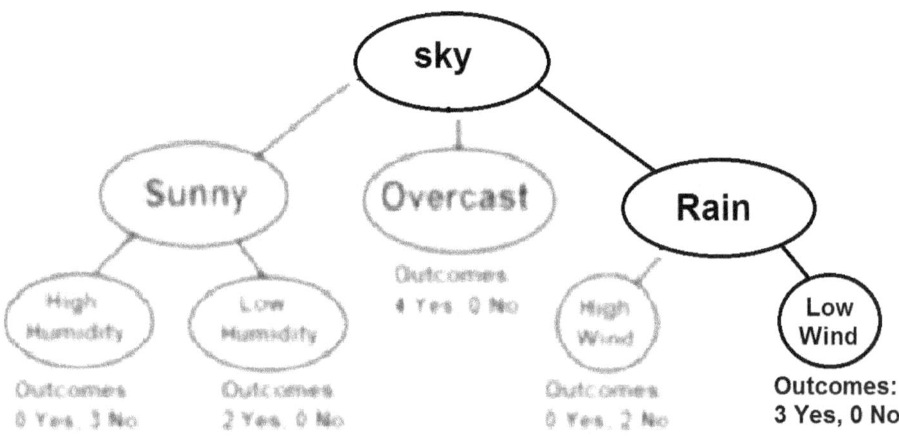

The given predictors lead us to a final subset containing 3 yes and 0 No – therefore we can make a final prediction: *Yes, John will play tennis today.*

Terminology

I hope this example gave you a practical understanding for decision tree algorithms and how they can solve real-life classification problems. In the following section I will dive deeper into the theoretical principles behind the algorithm. Let's define some key terminology:

Root Node - This is the node that contains all our training data. It is the starting point of every decision tree algorithm.

Decision Node – When a note splits your dataset based on a given predictor, it is called a decision node. It is forcing you to decide how to rearrange your dataset.

Leaf/Terminal Node: These are the final nodes in your tree, i.e. the leaves. They contain the smallest and most refined subsets.

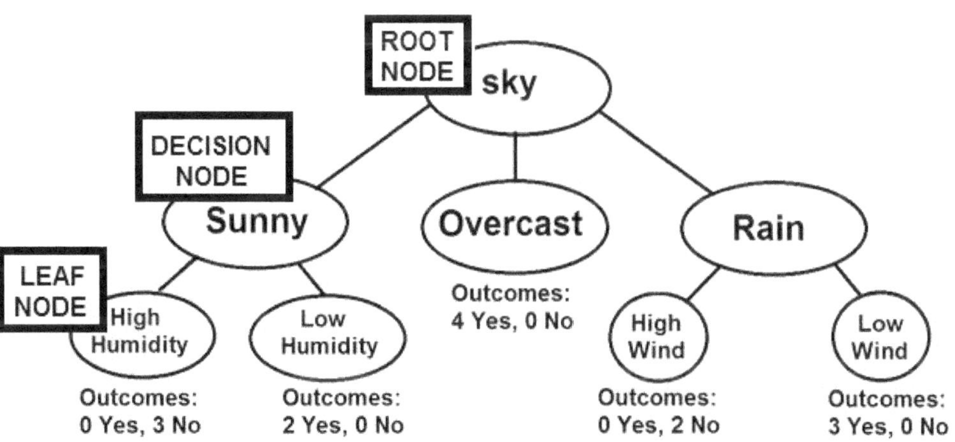

Splitting – This is the process of dividing a large set of data into smaller subsets. The main goal of this process is to *create subsets containing only one class of outcomes.*

Pruning: This process is the opposite of splitting. Pruning occurs when we remove the sub-nodes of a decision node. In the example below I have 'pruned' the decision nodes 'sunny' and 'Rain'.

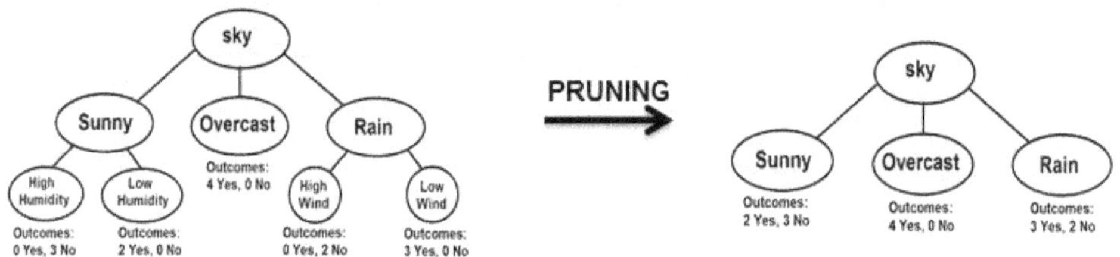

Branch/Subtree: A subsection of your main decision tree is called a *branch* or *subtree.*

Entropy/Disorder: If you are familiar with the fundamental laws of thermodynamics, you will already have come across of entropy – or disorder. In the context of Decision Tree algorithms, entropy is a measure of *how disordered or random the subset is at a particular node.* Entropy can be quantified using complex mathematical formulas, although I have deemed these beyond the scope of the book.

Information Gain: Information gain is the process of removing entropy (or randomness) from a Decision Tree. This means improving the quality/structure of data in your subsets.

Minimize Entropy, Maximize Information Gain

When you are building a decision tree classification model, I described your objective in the following way: *"obtain subsets that contain only one class of outcomes"*. Now, we can redefine this objective using more technical and appropriate language: your goal is *"to minimize entropy and maximize information gain."* Let's analyse the entropy found in our earlier example.

Node	Type	Subset	Distribution	entropy
sky	Root Node	10 yes, 3 No		**HIGH** The subset has no defined class, it is split between Yes and No – there is no clear answer.
Rain	Decision Node	3 Yes, 2 No		**HIGHER** There was no information gain from the root node; in fact there was *information loss*. Entropy has increased because this contains a more random distribution of YES and NO outcomes.
Low Wind	Leaf Node	3 Yes, 0 No		**ZERO** In this leaf node there is zero randomness. The entire subset has a single class – they are 100% 'YES'. There was a lot of information gain from the decision node.
High Wind	Leaf Node	0 Yes, 2 No		**ZERO** In this leaf node there is zero randomness. The entire subset has a single class – they are 100% NO. There was a lot of information gain from the decision node.

Final Remarks

The Decision Tree algorithm can produce very useful classification models. Today's machine learning engineers can access many classification algorithms with superior accuracy and reliability, however Decision Trees remain extremely popular. This is because Decision Trees are extremely easy to read and understand – an ideal choice for presentations, data exploration and visualizing the decision-making process of your algorithm. Finally, whenever you build a Decision Tree always remember your objective: *minimize entropy, maximize information gain.*

Chapter 9 – Support Vector Machines

Introduction

In earlier chapters we covered a number of machine learning algorithms including KNN, Naïve Bayes, Logistic Regression and Decision Trees. In this chapter we will focus on Support Vector Machines (SVM).

Think of these algorithms as weapons in an armory. The algorithms we have covered thus far represent large swords and heavy axes: they can chop through a lot of data quickly and are easy to use, but their cuts are not precise. In the same scenario, SVM represents a sharp cutting knife – it can cut only through a small amount of data and requires a lot of practice, but achieves a very high precision and accuracy.

Please note that SVM is a complex algorithm and relies on complex mathematical formulas. For this reason, I will focus only on the high-level concepts of the algorithm. I believe that an in-depth discussion covering all mathematical equations, derivations and implementation details for developers would go beyond the scope of this book.

Due to its complexity, SVM carries very high computational requirements – it also does not fare well with large datasets. If your training data contains tens of thousands of entries, SVM may not be your most appropriate choice.

What are Support Vector Machines?

SVM is a powerful machine learning algorithm used for *classification*. This algorithm searches for the **best** line that separates all different classes in your training data. In other words, it looks for the widest channel, street, gap (known as *hyperplane*) that creates the greatest separation (known as *margin*) between the classes of your data. The figure below illustrates these concepts:

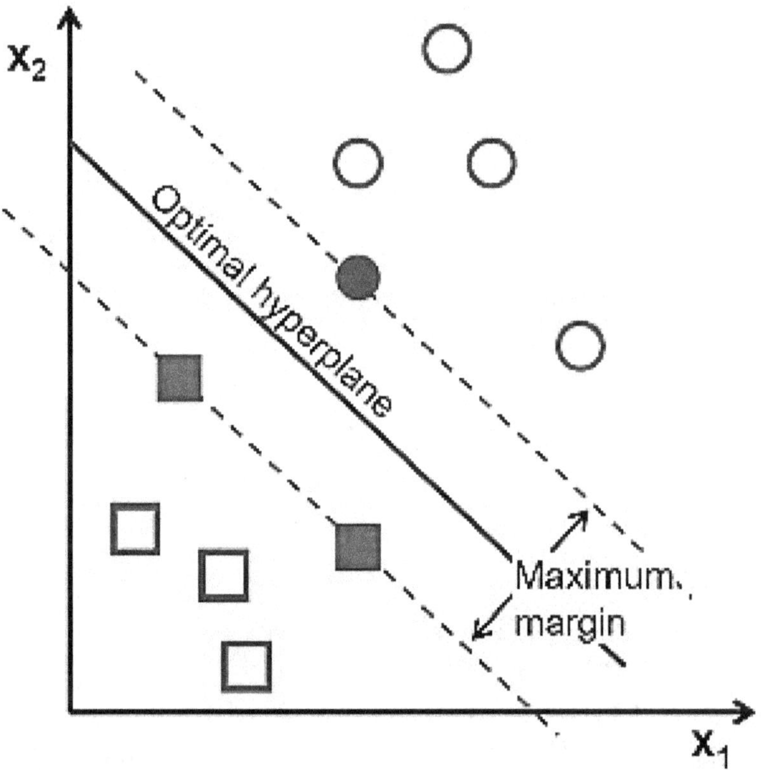

Note that the dimensionality of the data is not limited – i.e. your training data could be plotted on a 2-dimensional graph (2 predictors) or a 3-dimensional graph (3 predictors). The focus of this chapter is to explain *how SVM work* – for this reason I will only consider 2-dimensional cases as they are easier to visualize and understand. Please do keep in mind: in 2d the training data is separated by a line, while in 3d the training data is separated using a **plane** – think of it as a sheet or a wall separating the data.

Support Vector Machines in Practice

In the above section we have discussed the fundamental of SVMs: *finding the hyperplane that separates two classes of data with the greatest margin.* However, I believe this particular concept is best understood by means of practical examples and not discussion - so, let's dive right in.

In the following section I have assembled a variety of examples – these illustrate the fundamental rules you must consider when building SVMs on a new set of training data.

Rule 1 – Always separate as many class members as possible

In the example below **B** is the correct hyperplane because it separates all members of the two classes. Remember, maximum class separation is your first priority when working with SVM.

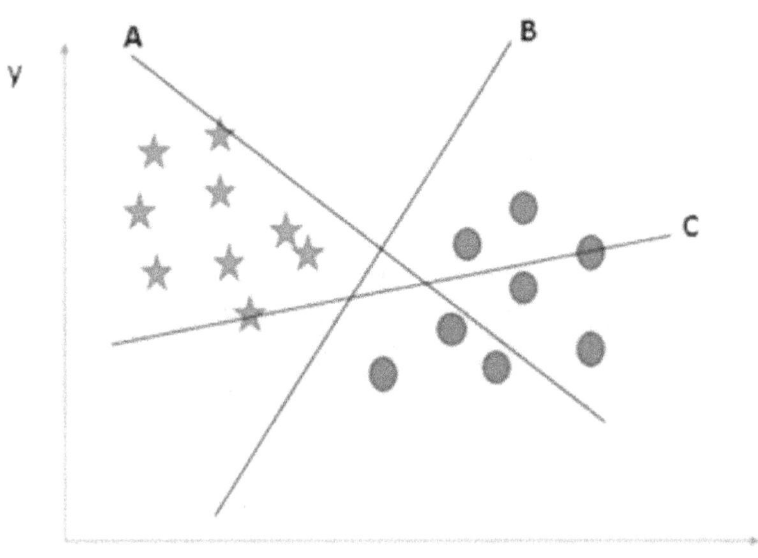

Rule 2 – Always Maximize Margin

Margin is the distance between your hyperplane and your closest data point. It is a measure of how well separated your classes are. When working with SVMs, you always want to maximize this distance. This builds a more robust and structured boundary. In the example found in the following page, "**C**" is the best hyperplane because it is furthest from your training data – and thus achieves the greatest margin.

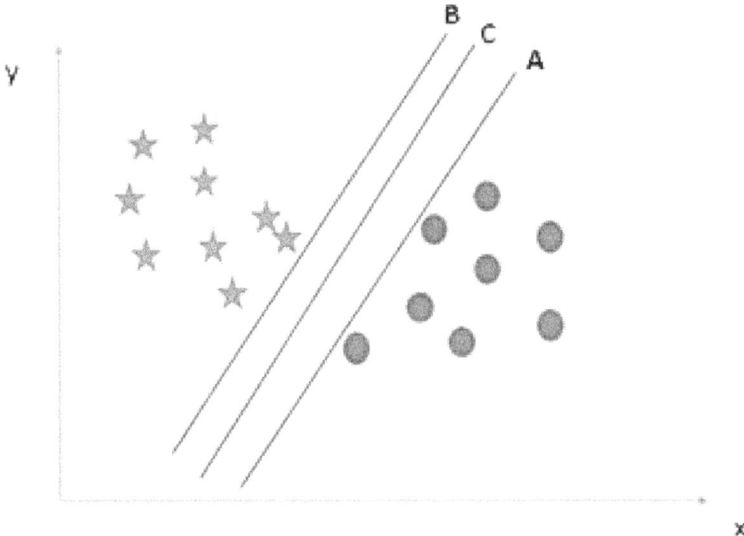

Rule 3 – Separation first, Margin second

It is important to maximize margin whenever possible, but maximum class separation is your first priority. In the example on page 52 you choose hyperplane "A" – even with a dramatically smaller margin, this hyperplane achieves full class separation and therefore should be selected.

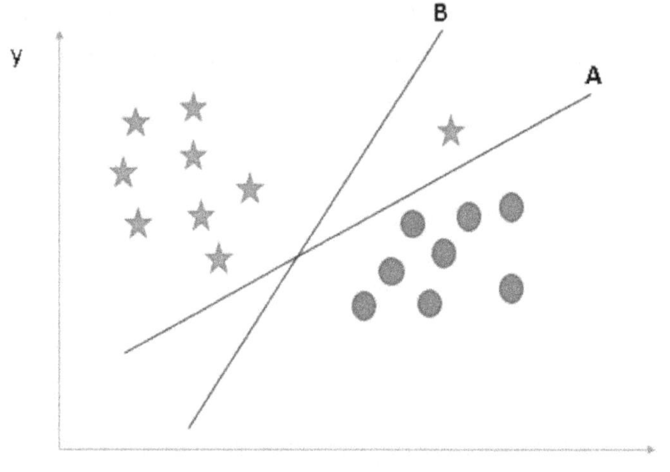

Rule 4 – Outliers exist!

In these examples we are working with very small and neat training data – real data is not. You will come across data sets with hundreds of entries, bad readings, mistakes and often with absolutely no visible structure. At times, you will find data that contains outliers and unfortunately you cannot do anything. That's perfectly fine, most SVM algorithms have built-in features to ignore these outliers... take a look at the example in the following page:

The Kernel Trick

Very often, you will come across data that is not linearly separable. In other words, you will not be able to separate two classes of data using a single straight-line or a flat-plane. Kernels are used to solve these problems.

Kernels are very complicated algebraic formulas that transform your data into linearly separable entities. Once the optimum algebraic equation is found, you can invert it to separate the original set of data. Take a look at the following example

Step 1 – You come across a dataset that is not linearly separable. The following dataset cannot be separated using a straight line.

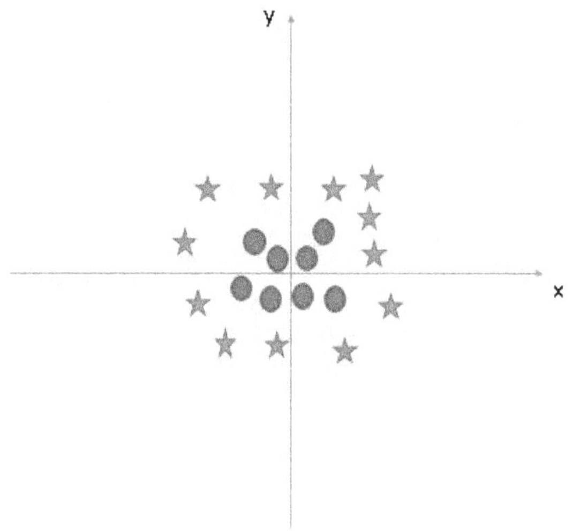

Step 2 – Apply a Kernel. For non-linearly-separable datasets, you can apply a kernel that transforms your data using complex geometrical equations. Once you find the function that matches your data distribution, you will obtain a linearly separable dataset. For example, I have converted the dataset above using a radial Kernel (i.e. when your data follow a circular pattern). *Please note: if your data has no structure or is simply random, you cannot produce a linearly separable set of data using a kernel.*

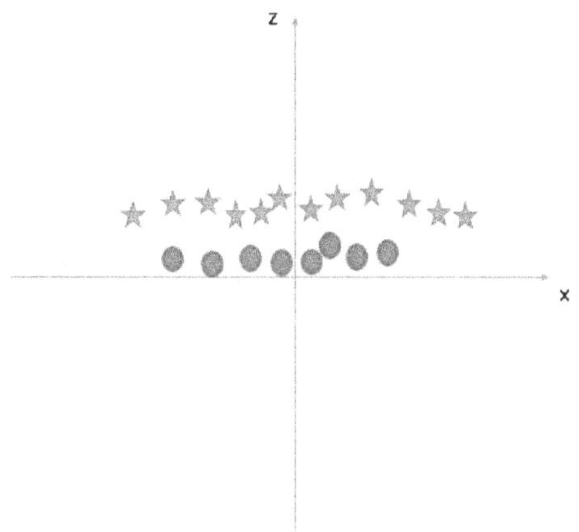

Step 3 – Inverse Kernel function to obtain a hyperplane on your original graph. Once you obtain a linearly-separable dataset, you can inverse the kernel and get a hyperplane that binds the data on your original graph, as shown below.

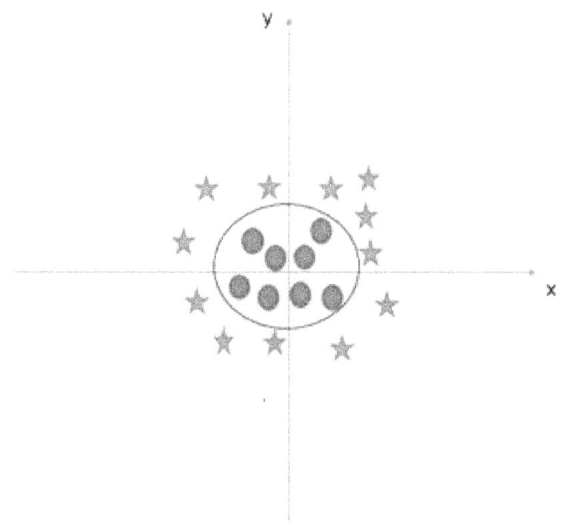

Where can I find Kernel equations?

I have explained that kernels are complicated algebraic functions; therefore you wonder where to find them. Do not worry about this, they are typically readily available and already implemented in most machine learning coding environments. You will have to select the most appropriate Kernels to suit your data and, as always, carry out parameter tuning for the best results.

With regards to coding environments, I highly recommend **Scikit** for data analysts who are familiar with Python (a popular computer programming language, especially among data scientists and machine learning engineers).

Chapter 10 – Neural Networks

Neural Networks are the most powerful group of machine learning algorithms, but also the most complex.

What Are Neural Networks?

Neural Networks are complex and powerful computational models derived directly from the structure and processes of our very own brains – downright to the individual brain cells, called **neurons.** They can be used to solve complex problems, but were never explicitly programmed to do so – these networks **learn how to solve problems.** Due to their complexity, it is difficult to describe Neural Networks in a few simple words – here's my best guess:

"Neural networks are a simplified model of our own human brain"

In fact, on the most fundamental level our brains and neural networks do the same job: both receive input signals, process these signals through a network of neurons and then emit an output signal. Of course, there are differences in execution, but the fundamental process is unchanged:

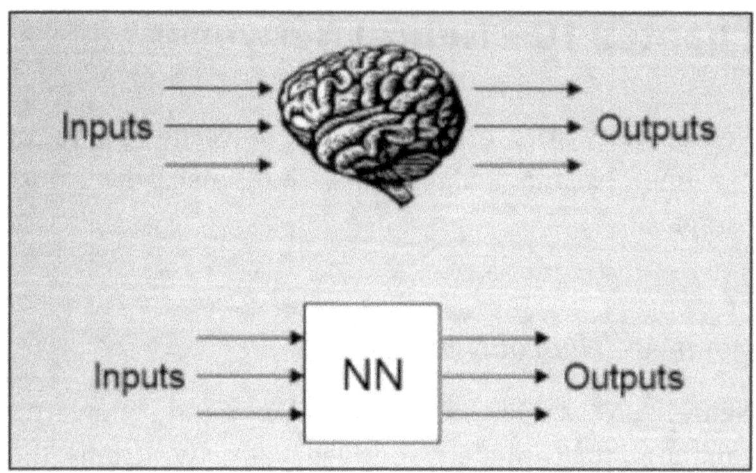

The similarities do not stop here, the structure of Neural Networks mimics our brains to a much greater degree – downright to individual brain cells. In fact, Neural Networks are built using a number of *Artificial Neurons* arranged into layers. Just like our brains, these are interconnected to each other and exchange signals with one another using *synapses*.

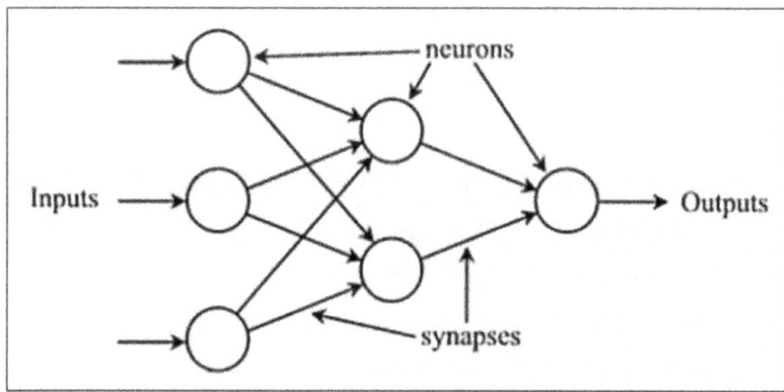

Training the Neural Network

Before a neural network can be used, it must learn how to solve problems – this occurs during training. Here is the main breakdown of the process:

1. Build a training data set (collect data samples representative of the average population)
2. **Input** the data into the network
3. The network will produce an **output** value
4. For each problem, an **error value** is calculated
5. Modify the **weights** of all artificial neurons
6. Continue training to **minimize error**
7. Once training has stopped, **test the network** to verify its accuracy
8. Use the network

Why do we use Neural Networks?

There are two particular features that make this tool so powerful:

1. *They can learn*: In the past, when engineers were faced with a new problem, they studied it, found a solution and afterwards built a program to implement the solution – with Neural Networks it's the complete opposite. Nowadays, engineers build machine capable of solving any problem and when a new problem arises the machine studies it, learns how to solve it and only then it finds a solution.
2. *They can adapt*: Once a Neural Network learns a process, it can adapt to completely new and

unexpected data. Old programs were extremely rigid – developers specify an input format and if the data does not match, then the program crashes and there is no solution. However, Neural Networks can adapt to data no one had ever seen before or search pictures nobody even knew existed.

Where do we use Neural Networks?

Neural Networks remain a relatively new technology in the industry and are yet to become mainstream. Yes, it is true that most electronics in our daily lives use machine learning algorithms, but only a few make use of Neural Networks. To date, they are used in only the most advanced applications at the forefront of the tech world, including:

- Natural Language processing: ex. Google Translator
- Pattern/Facial Recognition: ex. identifying faces in videos
- Targeted search & advertising

Conclusion

Dear Readers,

I sincerely thank you for reading until this point – I hope the information in this book has proved useful and interesting.

This book gave you an overview of today's most relevant machine learning algorithms, including KNN, Naïve Bayes, Logistic Regression, Decision Trees, Support Vector Machines and Neural Networks. For each algorithm we covered the fundamental concepts, most relevant mathematical formulas and its applications.

My Most Sincere Gratitude for Reading,

Morgan Maynard

BONUS CHAPTER – Modelling the Human Neuron (Extract from Book 2 of the Series)

Neurons are the most fundamental building blocks of our brain and billions of them are connected to execute our thought processes. Their connections and structures are constantly changing, allowing us to learn and adapt to our surroundings. Let's examine the structure of this fantastic cell.

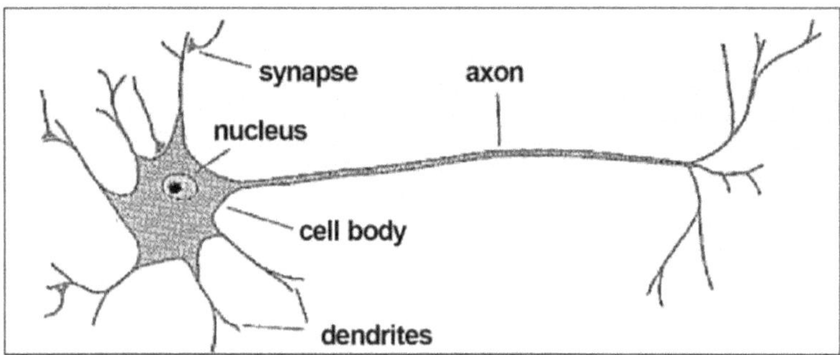

As you can tell, neurons have a main body and two branching sets of connections: the input structure (dendrites) and the output structure (the axon). The axons connect to the dendrites of other neurons via the synapse, hence forming a connection.

Signals are transmitted between neurons in the form of electro-chemical signals. A neuron first receives a signal via the dendrite to the cell body – the signal is processed, altered and assessed by the nucleus. However, the neuron will be activated only if the input signals exceed a certain amount within a short period (i.e. the threshold). If this amount is reached, the neuron becomes activated and it fires a signal to the attached neurons via the axons. This is how neurons are interconnected and exchange information.

Artificial Neurons

Now that we have examined the basic structure of a neuron, we can investigate how to model its functions and operation using software. We create artificial neurons as relatively simple mathematical functions – their *output* is calculated using three main factors:

- *Input signals*: these originate directly from neighboring neurons.
- *Weights*: each neuron applies a unique weighting factor to every input signal received.
- *Bias*: this value is unique to the neuron and is applied to the overall output.

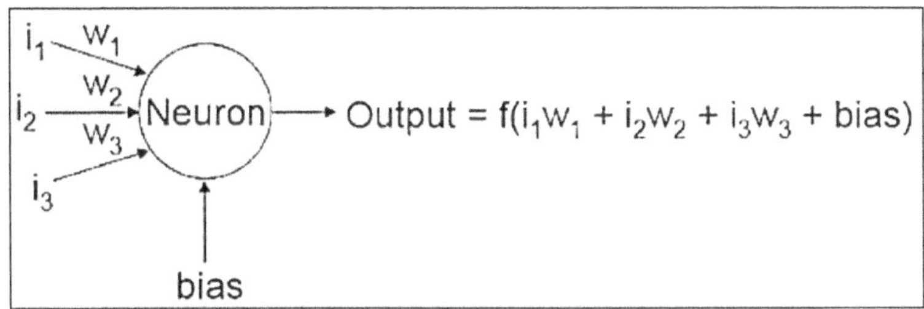

Notice that the output is not the simple sum of all the weights, it must be multiplied by an activation function. Most artificial neurons are modeled using a *sigmoid activation function*, as shown below. This is a smooth, continuous and always increasing curve (i.e. gradient is always positive). The mathematical equation of the sigmoid function is $f(x) = 1/(1 + e^{-x})$.

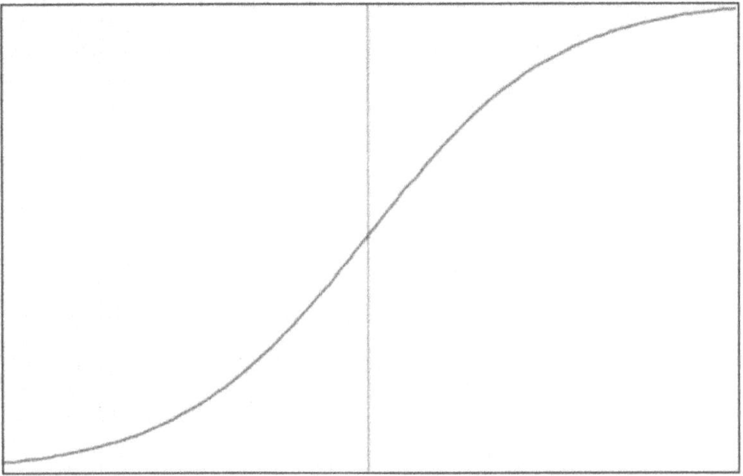

*Editor's note: this chapter was taken from the second instalment of the series "**Neural Networks: Introduction to Artificial Neurons, Backpropagation and Multilayer Feedforward Neural Networks**". You can find the full series on my official Amazon Author Page. Continue to grow your knowledge today!*